TO

FROM

Mom

you're some kinda' wonderful!

Detroit • New York

Mom you're some kinda' wonderful!

Copyright © 2007

Avanti Press, Inc.
Box 2656
Detroit, Michigan 48231

www.avantipress.com

ISBN: 193395762-X
07 08 09 APO 10 9 8 7 6 5 4 3 2 1
Printed in China

Mom

you're some kinda' wonderful!

Moms are some kind of wonderful in so many ways!

They're there for us from day one and keep us growing and learning as we move on in this life. They are the center of the family and the sail that keeps us moving through each day. While there is only one official calendar day set aside for celebrating Mom each year, we know it is every day that she contributes to our well-being and happiness.

Moms have

the answers to life's questions
and challenges. They might
not always be right,
but they're never wrong.

Moms love
to nurture natural talents.

Moms make sure

that the
little things are,
in fact, the
big things.

Moms also make sure
that there is enough icing...
...and two beaters.

Moms know that phases come and go and they let time take its course… without too much teasing.

Moms start

the day with a smile
and always see
...the sunny side...
unless the request
is for scrambled.

Moms know that looking good counts for something in the game of life.

Moms know

that it is rarely, if ever,
a good idea to say,
"Go ask your Dad."

Moms may

be outta sight
but they're never outta mind.

Moms and flowers

always go well
together because they make
those around them smile.

Moms can do anything
and everything because,
well, they're Moms.

Moms somehow

have the same handwriting as the "Secret Admirer."

Moms always know how to act surprised even when Dads give them lousy gifts.

Moms lead
by example.

Moms encourage

individuality
or learn to look
the other way.

Moms' "wisdom"

usually comes from experience.

Moms know

that there are a pair of
shoes for every occasion
and that style and
comfort can coexist.

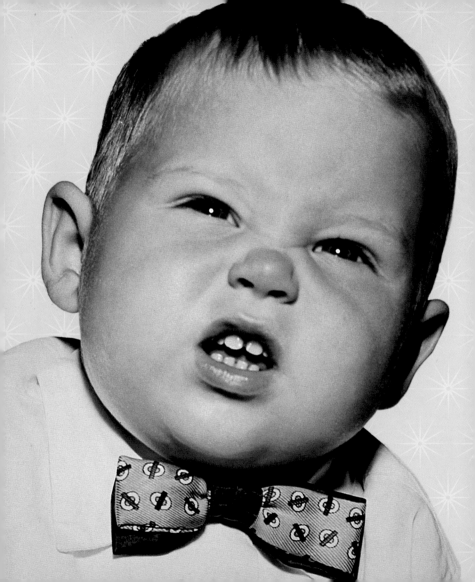

Moms know that taking
a goofy baby photo will come
in handy one day…

Moms never tire.

Mom, you're the best...

so here's a little something
for you to polish.

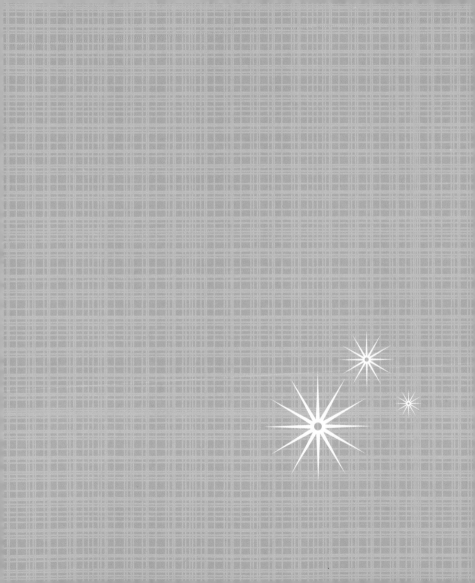